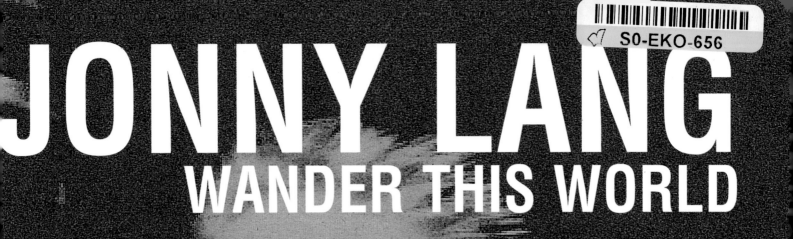

# JONNY LANG
## WANDER THIS WORLD

S0-EKO-656

Transcribed by DANNY BEGELMAN

Project Manager: JEANNETTE DE LISA
Music Editor: COLGAN BRYAN

Album Art: ©1998 A&M Records, Inc.
Album Art Direction and Design: KAREN WALKER
Album Photography: KEN SCHLES
Book Art Layout: LISA GREENE MANE

# CONTENTS

# STILL RAININ'

Words and Music by
BRUCE McCABE

Tune up 1/2 step:
⑥= E#  ③= G#
⑤= A#  ②= B#
④= D#  ①= E#

**Moderate rock** ♩ = 100

*Intro:*
**Gtr. 1** *(dist.)*
Piano, Bass, & Drums          N.C.          *E    G    A

**Gtr. 2** *(dist.)*

**Gtr. 3** *(dist.)*                         **Rhy. Fig. 1**

*Chord symbols reflect implied harmonies.

E    G    A    G    E    G

fill my eyes. __
love can bring. __
used to be. __

Well, I know by now she ain't com-in' back. __
It don't get no bet - ter with each pass-ing day. __
Her love shone on me just like the morn-ing light. __

w/**Fill 2** *(Gtr. 1) 3rd time*

*To Coda*

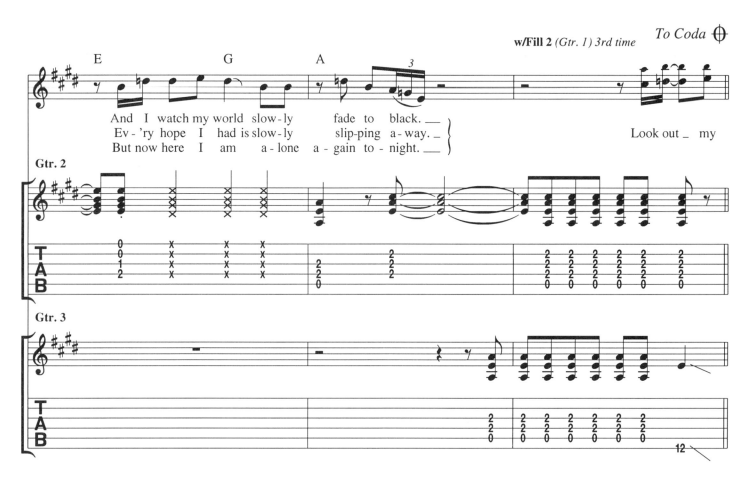

And I watch my world slow-ly fade to black. __
Ev-'ry hope I had is slow-ly slip-ping a - way. __
But now here I am a - lone a - gain to - night. __

Look out __ my

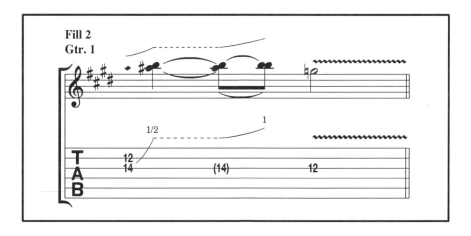

**Fill 2**
**Gtr. 1**

*Chorus:*
**w/Rhy. Fig. 1** *(Gtr. 3) simile*
**w/Fill 1** *(Gtr. 1) 2nd time*

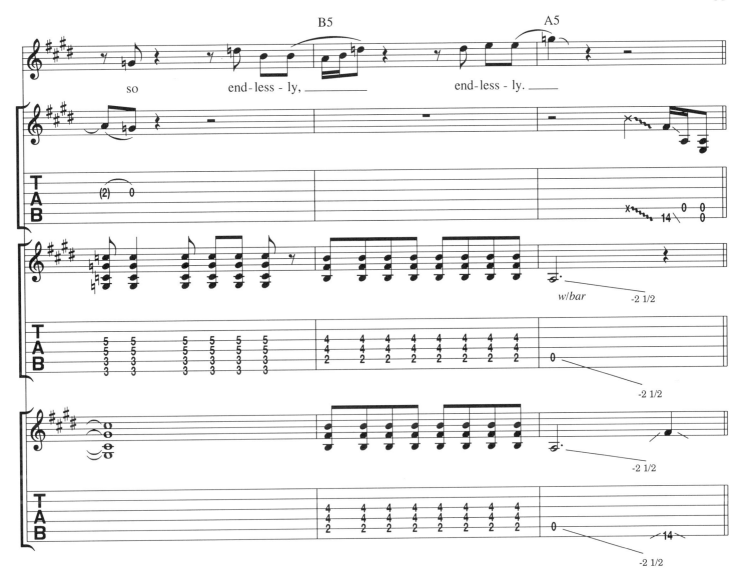

**Guitar Solo:**
**w/Rhy. Fig. 2** *(Gtr. 2) 1st 7 meas.*
**w/Rhy. Fig. 1** *(Gtr. 3) 1st 7 meas.*

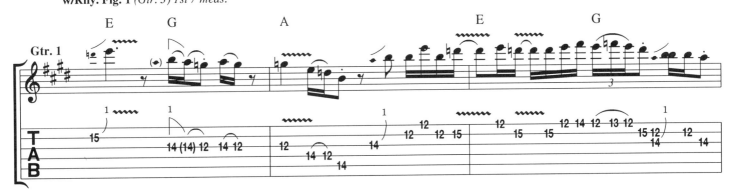

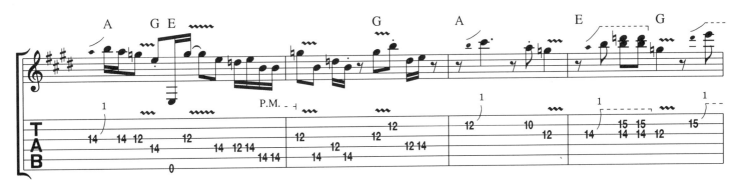

Still Rainin' – 11 – 6
PG9809

*Guitar Solo:*

# BREAKIN' ME

Words and Music by
JONNY LANG and KEVIN BOWE

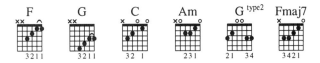

*Verse 1:*

**w/Rhy. Fig. 1** *(Gtr. 1) 2 times, simile*

'ry day _____ I see your face, I wish that I'd stayed. __

__ Don't e-ven know what made __ me run

a-way; it's just the way __ I __ play the game. __

*Verses 2 & 3:*

**w/Rhy. Fig. 1** *(Gtr. 1) simile*

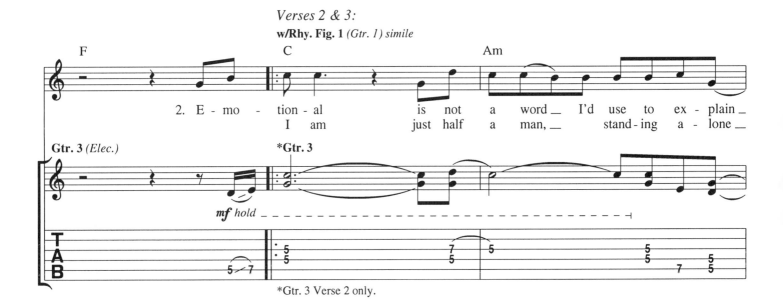

2. E-mo-tion-al is not a word __ I'd use to ex-plain __
I am just half a man, __ stand-ing a-lone __

**Gtr. 3** *(Elec.)*     **\*Gtr. 3**

*mf* hold _ _ _ _ _ _ _ _ _ _ _ _ _ _ _ _ _ _ _ _ _ _ _ _ _

*\*Gtr. 3 Verse 2 only.*

**w/Rhy. Fig. 1** *(Gtr. 1) 1st 3 meas. only, sim.*

__ my-self. __ But now you've got me down up-on my knees, oh, ba-
feel-ing like I lost my on-ly chance at hap-

hold _ _ _ _ _ _ _ _ _ _ _ _ _ _

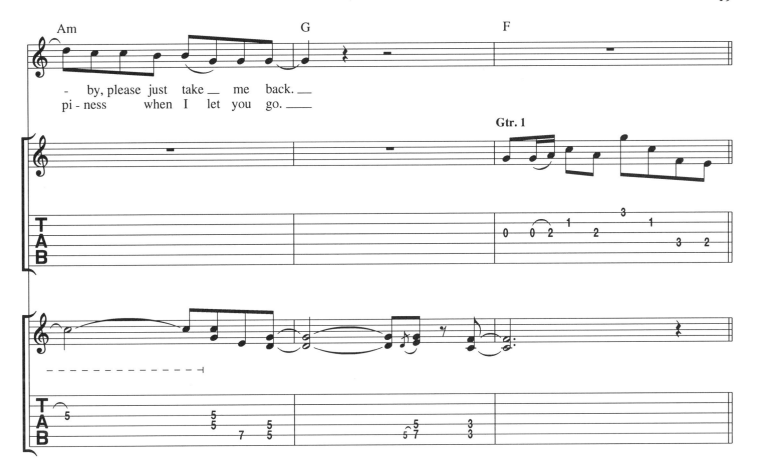

**Chorus 1 & 2:**

by, please just take ___ me back. ___
pi - ness when I let you go. ___

1. I ___ don't want ___ to be ___ in ___ love, ___ but you're mak-
2. I ___ don't want ___ to be a - lone, ___ think-in' 'bout ___

Breakin' Me – 9 – 3
PG9809

20

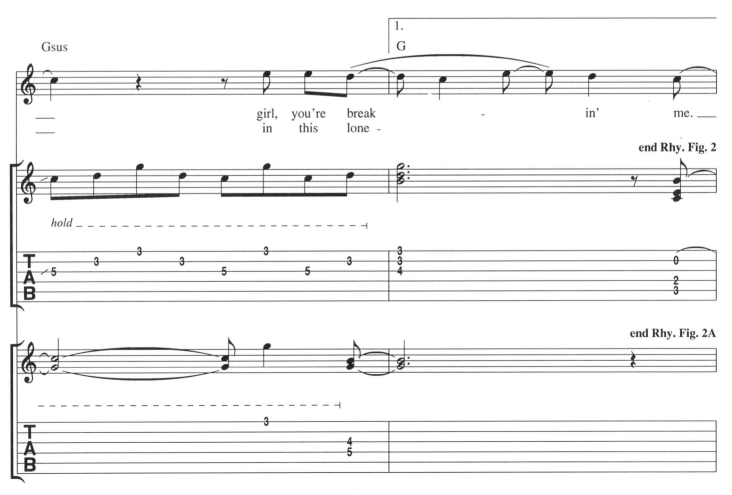

Breakin' Me – 9 – 4
PG9809

Am — G type2 — F — Cont. in notation

me in just one more time.

Gtr. 1

Gtr. 3

hold _ _ _ _ _

*Chorus 3:*
w/Rhy. Figs. **2** *(Gtr. 1)* & **2A** *(Gtr. 3) both 1st 4 meas. only, simile*

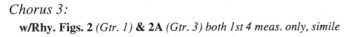

Dm — C — F

Well, I __ know you lost __ your faith __ in __ me, __ but I still __ be - lieve. __

w/Rhy. Figs. **2** *(Gtr. 1)* & **2A** *(Gtr. 3) both simile*

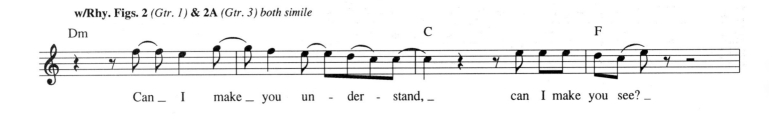

Dm — C — F

Can __ I make __ you un - der - stand, __ can I make you see? __

Dm — Gsus — G

I __ am des - p'rate for __ your __ love __ and it's break - in' __ me.

*Outro: w/ad lib. vocal*
**w/Rhy. Figs. 1** *(Gtr. 1)* **& 1A** *(Gtr. 2) both 5 times, simile*

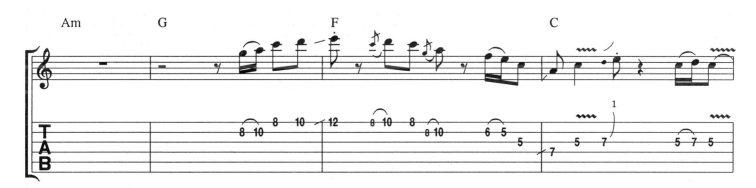

*Begin fade*

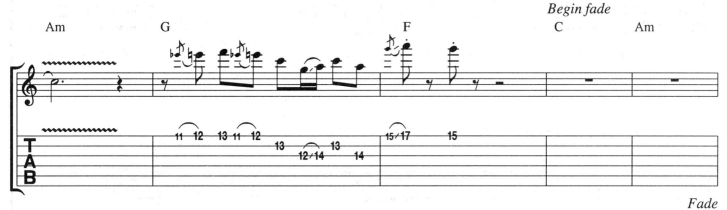

*Fade*
**w/Rhy. Figs. 1** *(Gtr. 1)* **& 1A** *(Gtr. 2) both 1st 2 meas. only*

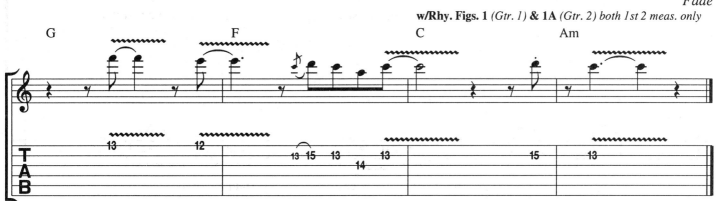

Breakin' Me – 9 – 9
PG9809

# SECOND GUESSING

Words and Music by
BRUCE McCABE and DAVID Z

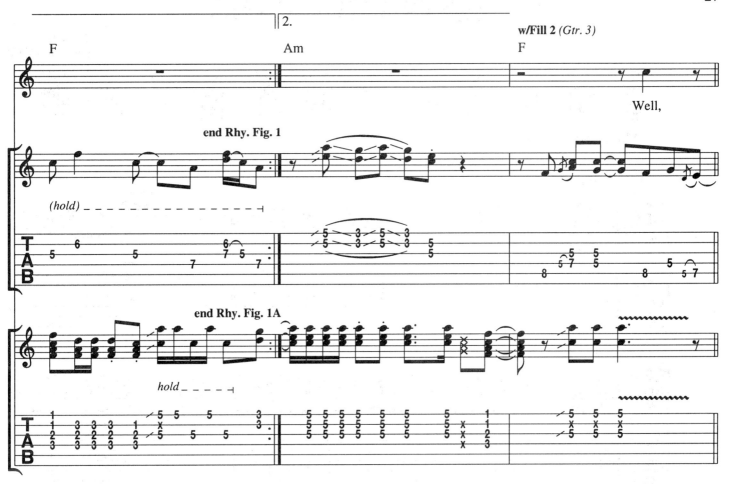

Verse 1:

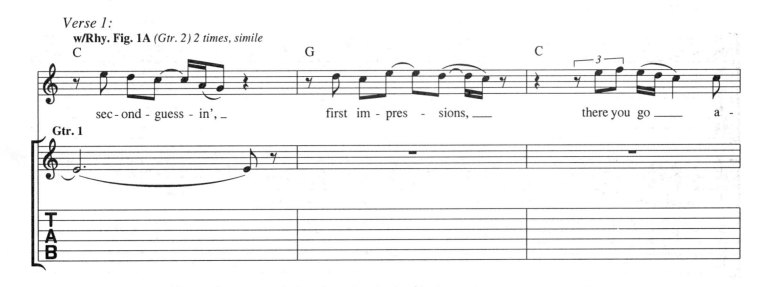

sec-ond - guess - in', _ first im - pres - sions, ___ there you go ___ a-

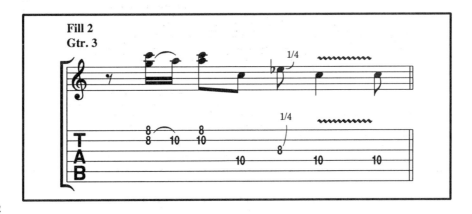

gain. ___          You're rush-ing off     in     all     di - rec - tions _

since I don't _ know when. _____          Well, all day long _ you've been build-

ing walls          and you've been     build-ing walls ____ all ____ day.     Put-ting ceil-

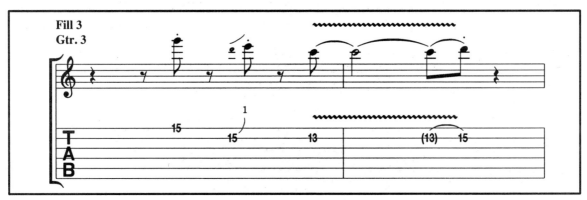

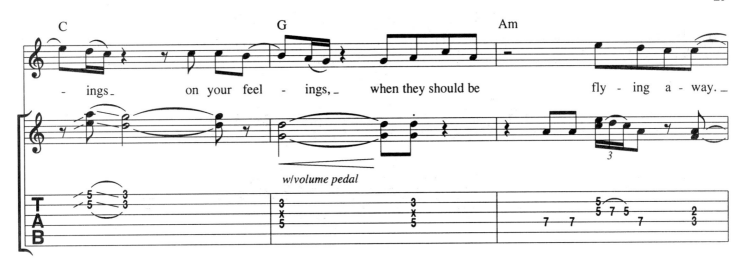

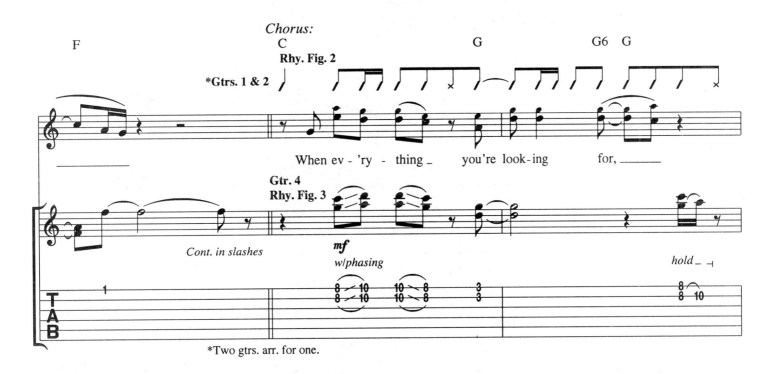

*Two gtrs. arr. for one.

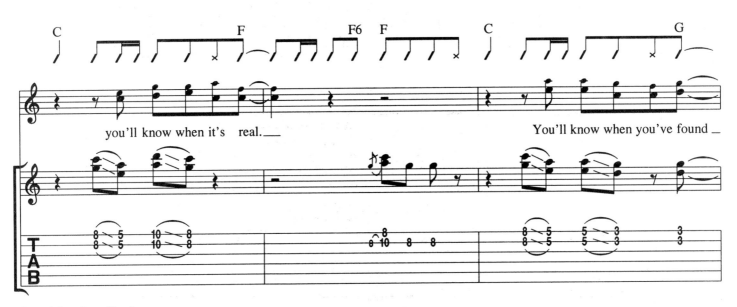

Your piece of pa-per flew out the win-dow. _____ You watched it __ try and land.

You felt so bad _____ as it flew out of sight, _

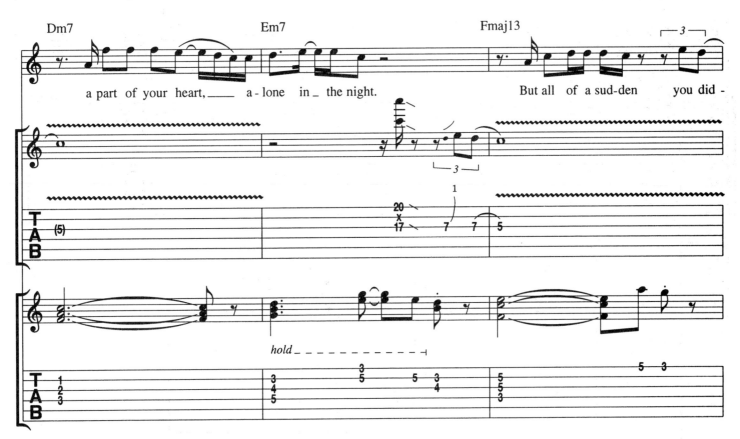

a part of your heart, _____ a-lone in _ the night. But all of a sud-den you did-

32

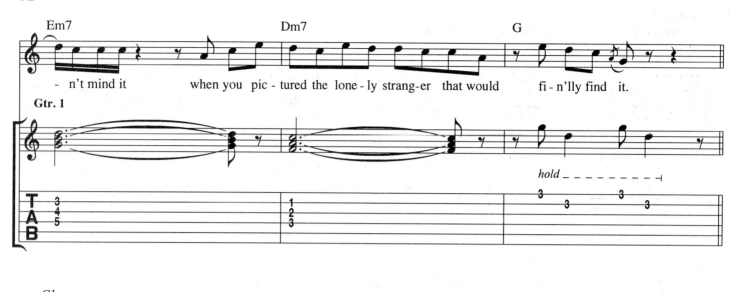

Chorus:

w/Rhy. Fig. 2 *(Gtrs. 1 & 2) 1st 7 meas. only, simile*

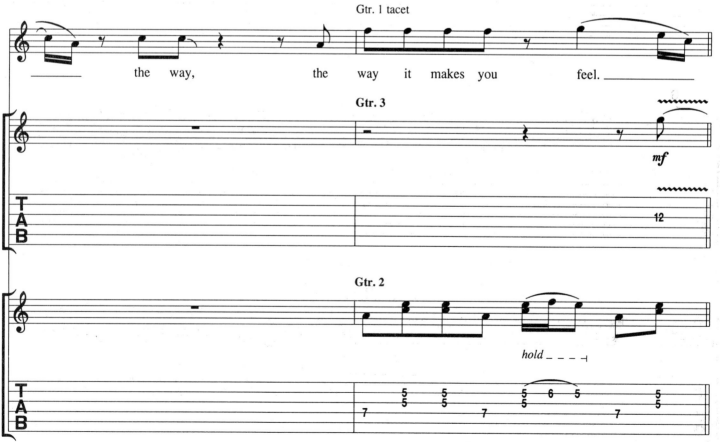

Guitar Solo:
w/Rhy. Figs. 1 *(Gtr. 1)* & 1A *(Gtr. 2)* both 2 times, simile

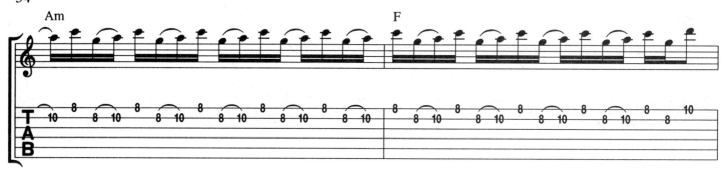

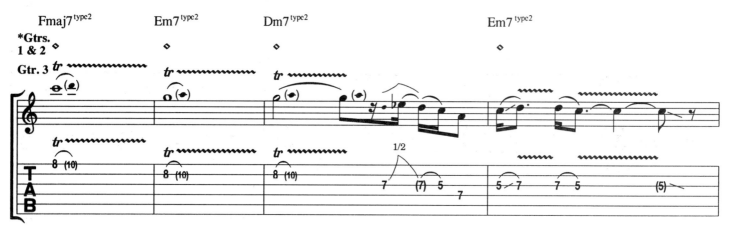

*Two gtrs. arr. for one.

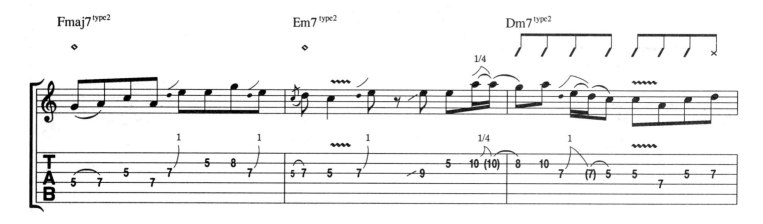

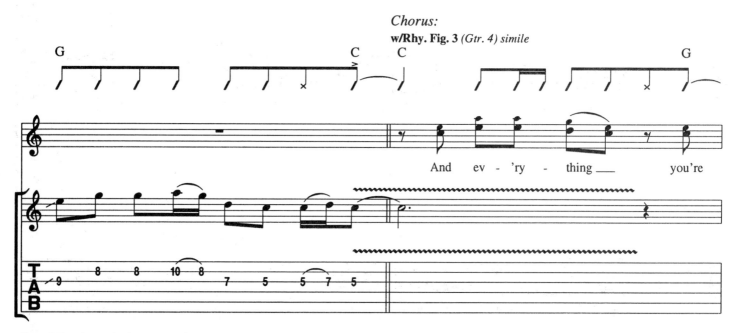

Gtr. 3 tacet

G6 G       C       F     F6 F

look-ing     for, __      you'll know  when it's real. _____

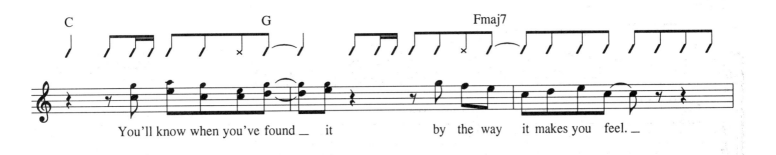

C       G       Fmaj7

You'll know when you've found _ it    by the way  it makes you feel. _

w/Rhy. Fig. 2 *(Gtrs. 1 & 2) simile*
w/Rhy. Fig. 3 *(Gtr. 4) simile*

C       G    G6 G

Ah,  ba - by.     Ev - 'ry - thing _ you're  look - ing   for, _____

C       F     F6 F

you  know _  it's  real. _____  (Yeah, ___  ba - by. _____)

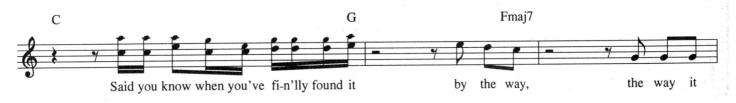

C       G      Fmaj7

Said you know when you've fi-n'lly found it    by the way,    the way it

# I AM

Words and Music by PRINCE,
LEVI SEACER, JR. and DAVID Z

**Moderate funk/blues**  ♩ = 96

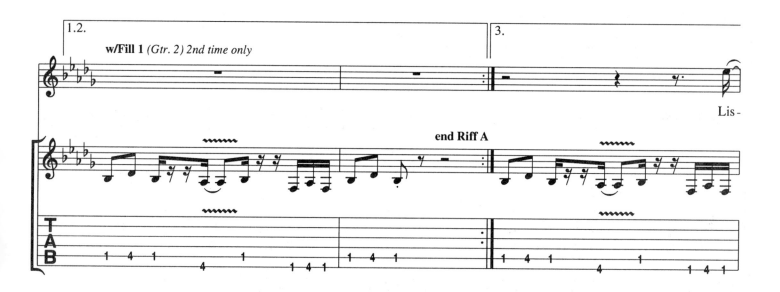

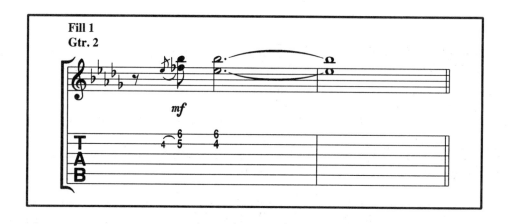

40

*Bridge:*

**w/Riff A** *(Gtr. 1) 4 times*

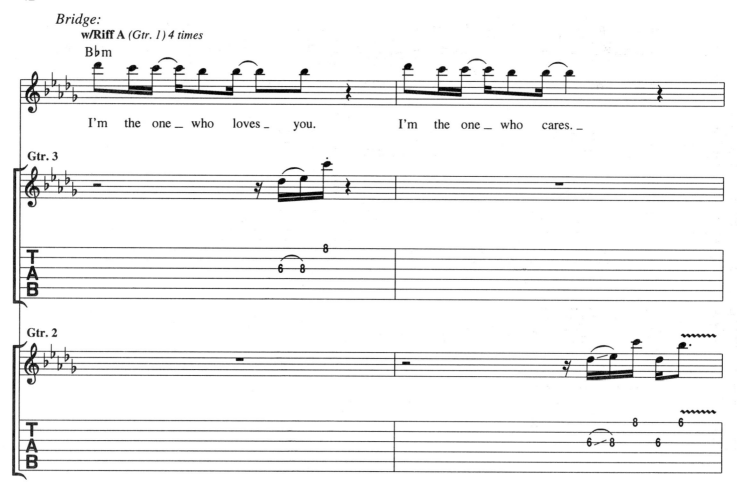

I'm the one — who loves — you.    I'm the one — who cares. —

You could fly — me to — the moon — if I — could find — you there. ———

All the rich - es in __ this world __ mean noth-ing with - out you here. __ Who-ev -

- er, what - ev - er, how - ev - er, when-ev - er you need me, I'll al - ways be __ here. __ Who-ev-

44

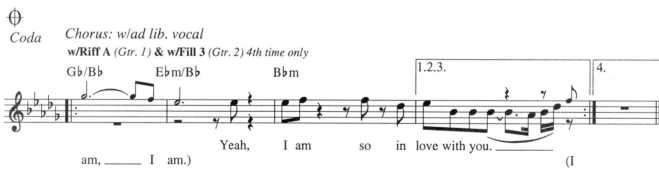

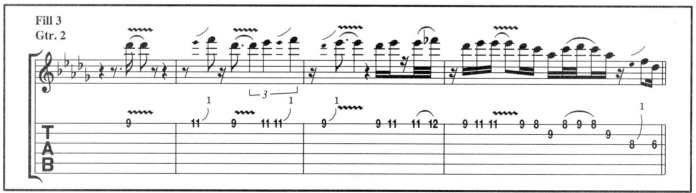

I Am – 8 – 7
PG9809

*Outro: w/ad lib. vocal*
  **w/Riff A** *(Gtr. 1) 4 times* **& w/Rhy. Fig. 1** *(Gtr. 3) 4 times, simile*

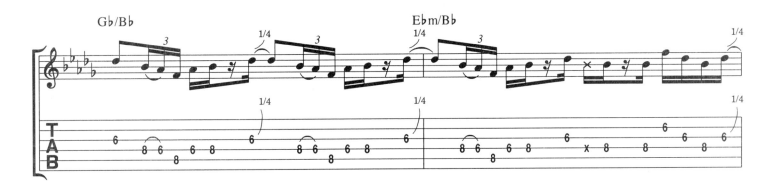

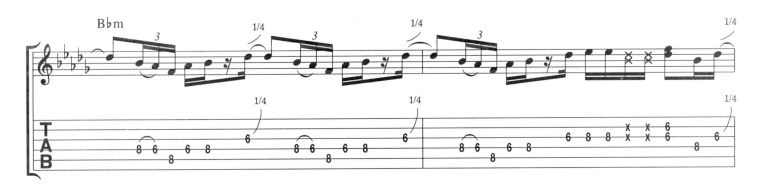

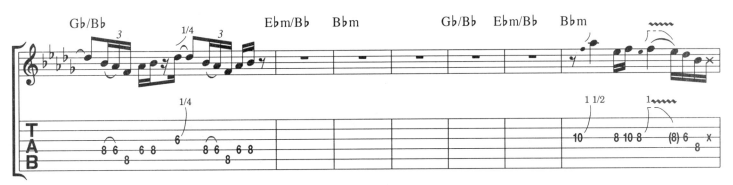

*Begin fade*    **w/Riff A** *(Gtr. 1) 1st 2 meas. only*    *Fade*
        **& w/Rhy. Fig. 1** *(Gtr. 3) 1st 2 meas. only, simile*

# WANDER THIS WORLD

Words and Music by
PAUL DIETHELM and BRUCE McCABE

*Dobro arr. for gtr. Play w/capo at 5th fret. Music is written at concert pitch: Tab numbers depict fingerings relative to capo.

Wander This World – 16 – 1
PG9809

48

*Chorus:*

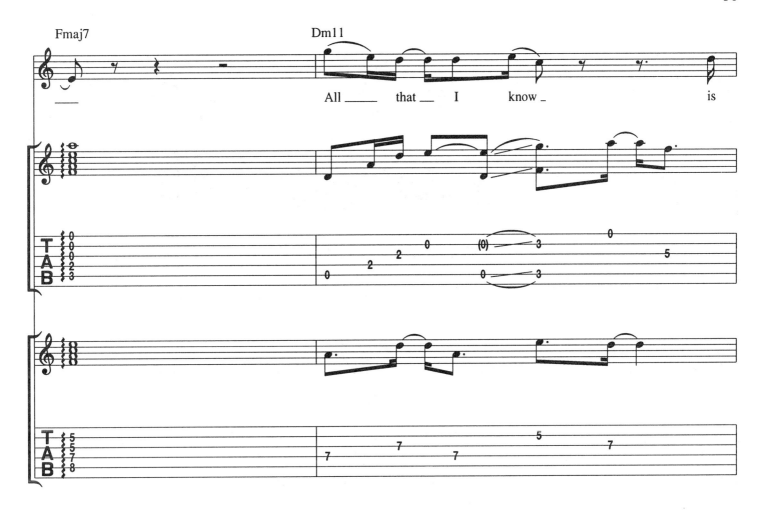

52

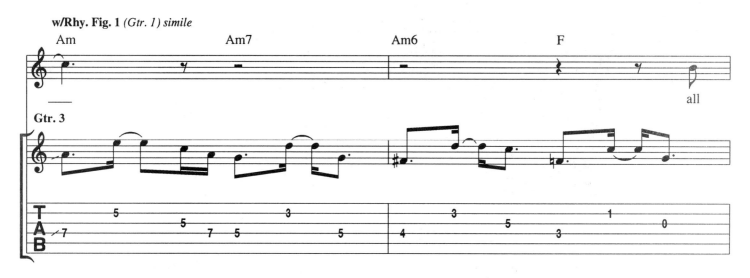

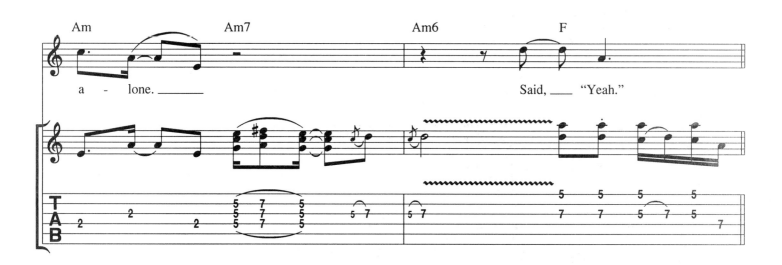

*Guitar Solo:*

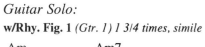

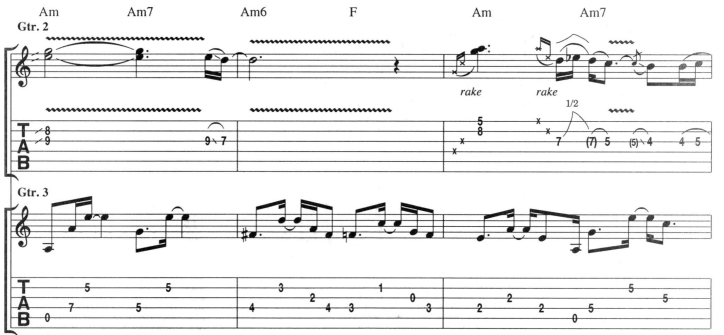

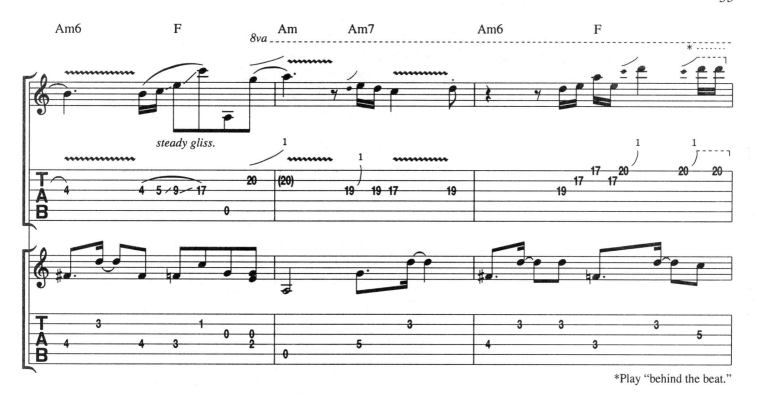

*Play "behind the beat."

**w/Rhy. Fill 1** *(Gtr. 1)*

*Bridge:*
**w/Rhy. Fig. 3** *(Gtr. 1) simile*

*Vibrato causes open 3rd string to sound.

60

# WALKING AWAY

Words and Music by
JONNY LANG and JERRY LYNN WILLIAMS

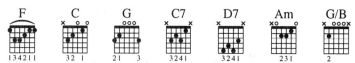

**Moderately slow** ♩ = 58

*Intro:*

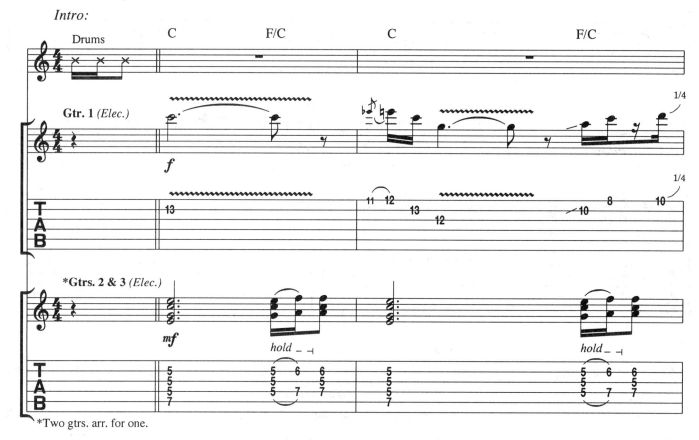

*Two gtrs. arr. for one.

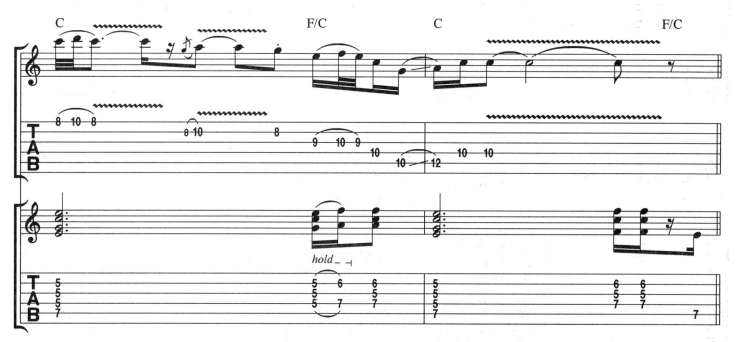

Walking Away – 8 – 1
PG9809

Walking Away – 8 – 2
PG9809

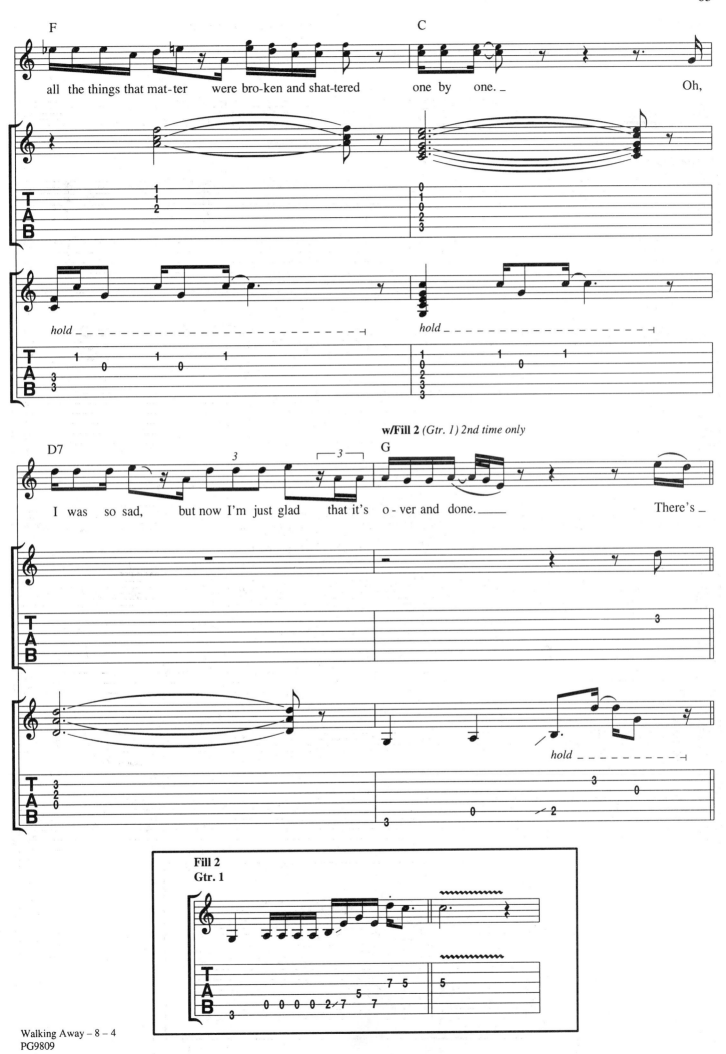

all the things that mat-ter were bro-ken and shat-tered one by one. \_ Oh,

I was so sad, but now I'm just glad that it's o-ver and done.\_\_ There's \_

w/Fill 2 *(Gtr. 1) 2nd time only*

Fill 2
Gtr. 1

66

*Chorus:*
*Gtr. 4 cont. rhy. simile*

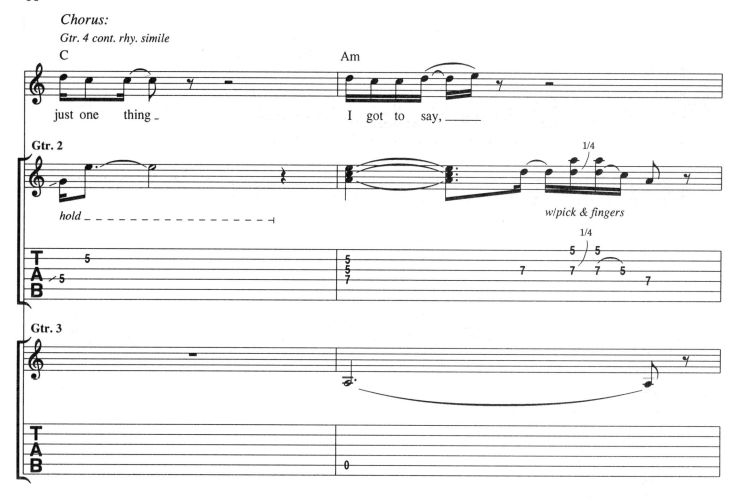

just one thing _      I got to say, _____

**Gtr. 2**

*hold* _ _ _ _ _ _ _ _ _ _ _ _ _ ⌐

*w/pick & fingers*

**Gtr. 3**

I tru - ly loved _ you,      but now I'm walk-ing a - way. _      Yeah, _

*hold* _ _ ⌐

68

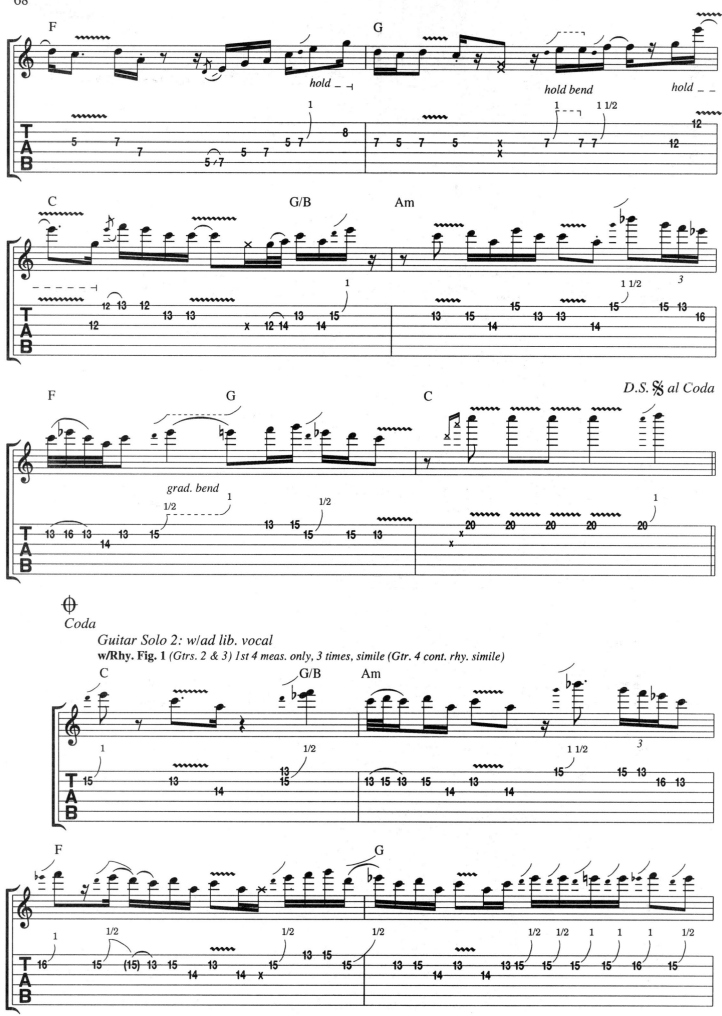

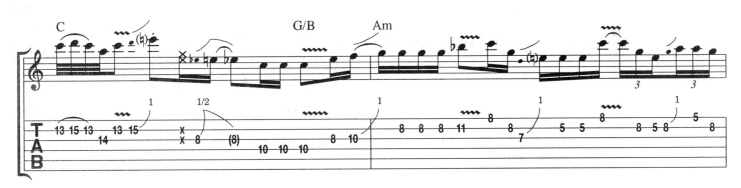

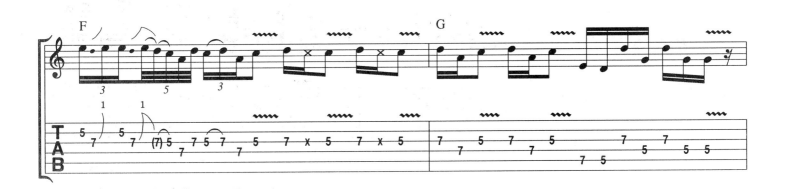

*Begin fade*

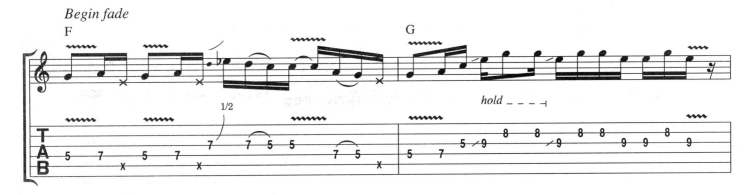

**w/Rhy. Fig. 1** *(Gtrs. 2 & 3) 1st meas. only, simile*

*Fade*

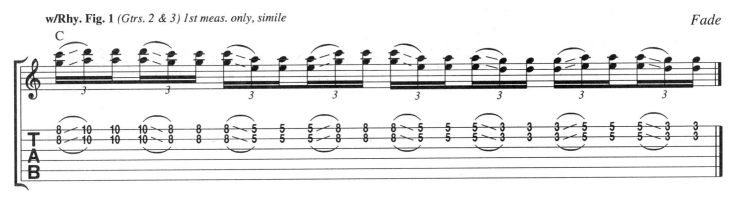

Walking Away – 8 – 8
PG9809

# THE LEVEE

Words and Music by
JONNY LANG and KEVIN BOWE

*Chord names reflect Gtr. 3 (see frames).

The Levee – 9 – 1
PG9809

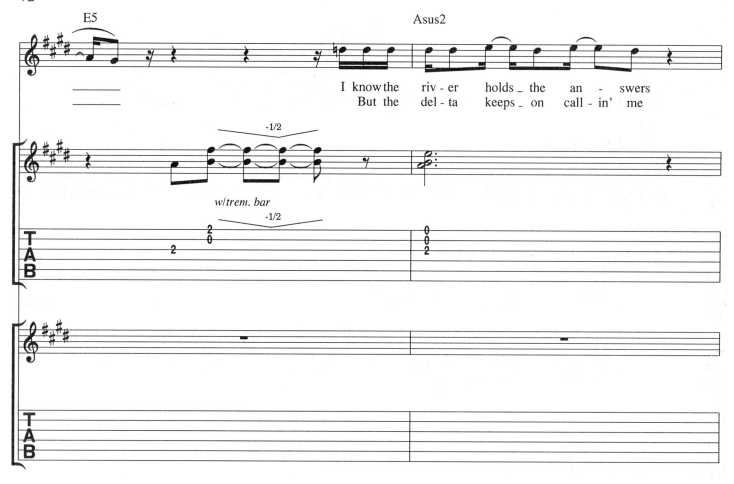

I know the riv-er holds _ the an - swers
But the del - ta keeps _ on call - in' me

to the ques-tions in __ my mind. _____ Ow, ___ no mat -
no mat - ter what I do, _____

**Gtr. 4** *(Elec., left)*

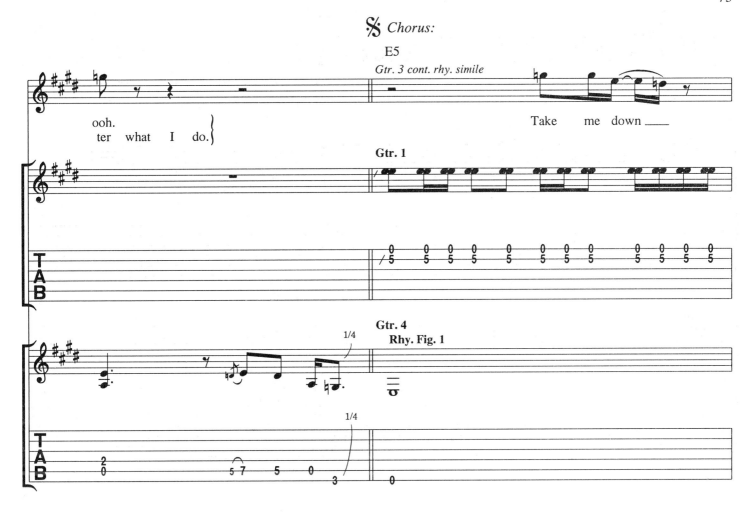

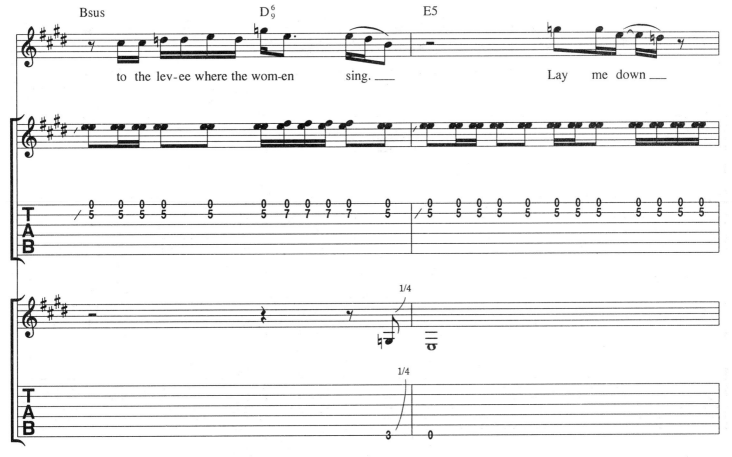

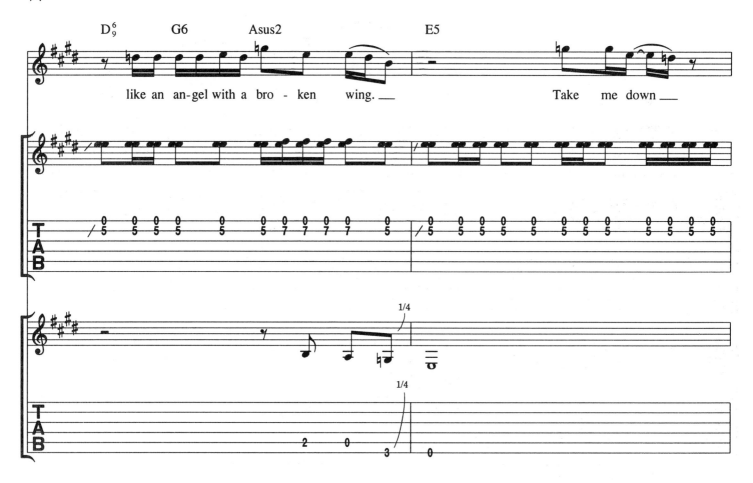

like an an-gel with a bro-ken wing. \_\_\_ Take me down \_\_\_

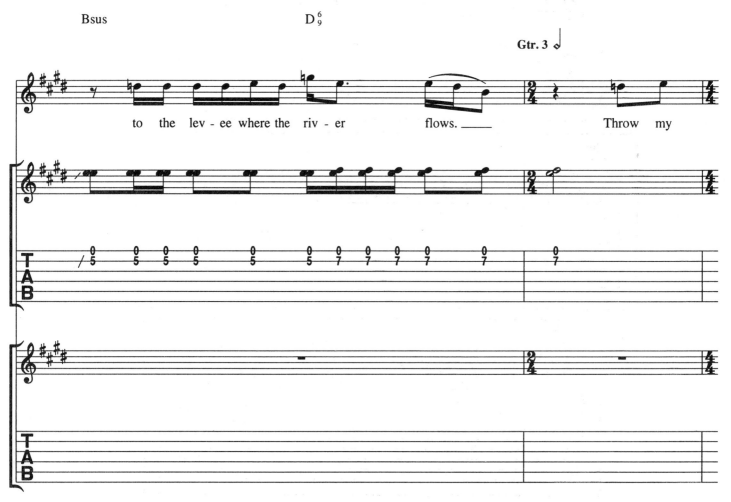

Gtr. 3

to the lev-ee where the riv-er flows. \_\_\_ Throw my

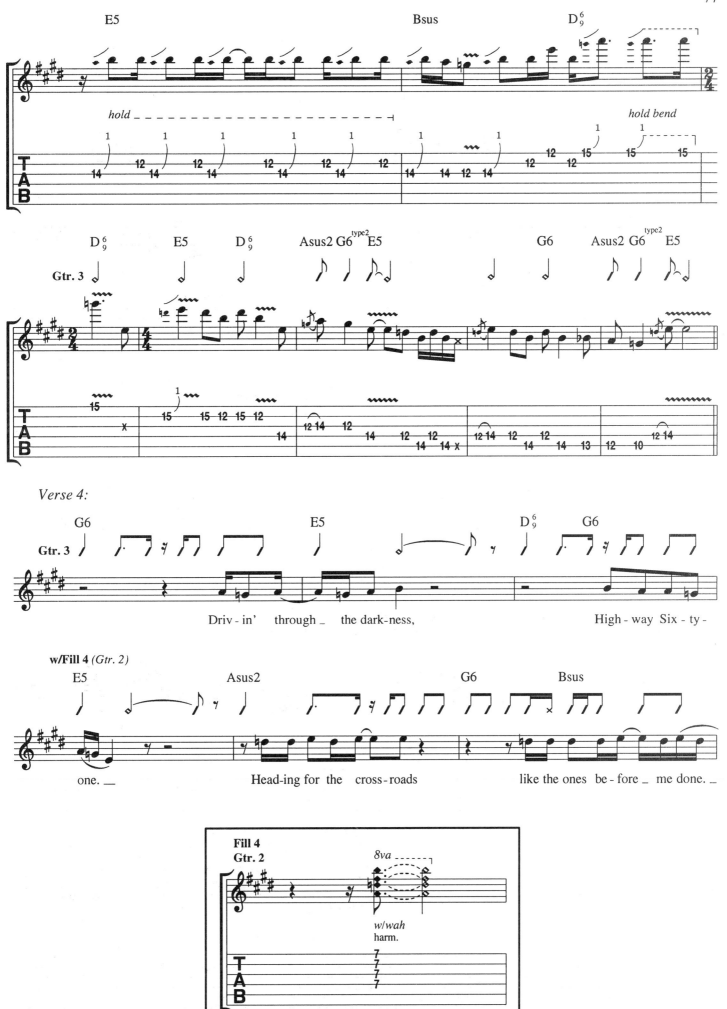

Verse 4:

Driv - in' through _ the dark-ness,    High - way Six - ty -

one. _    Head-ing for the cross-roads    like the ones be - fore _ me done. _

78

The Levee – 9 – 9
PG9809

# ANGEL OF MERCY

Words and Music by
BRUCE McCABE and MICHAEL HENDERSON

**Moderately** ♩ = 80

*Intro:*

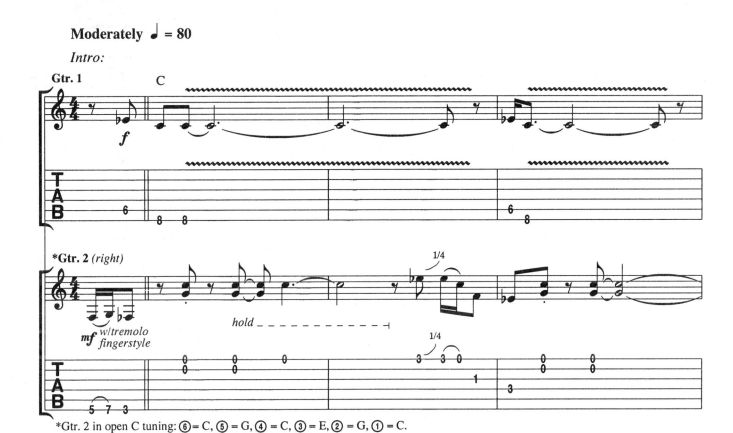

*\*Gtr. 2 in open C tuning: ⑥ = C, ⑤ = G, ④ = C, ③ = E, ② = G, ① = C.*

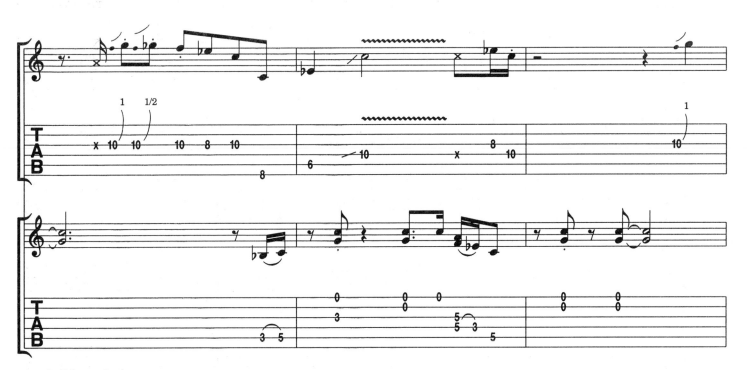

Angel of Mercy – 7 – 1
PG9809

%. *Verse:*
C

1. An - gel of mer - cy,
   when the shad - ows fall - in' and the
   some - times I feel a
4. Stay with me, ba - by,

*Gtr. 2

**Gtr. 2

*Gtr. 2 for Verses 1, 2, and 4 (simile on repeats).
**Gtr. 2 for Verse 3 only.

you don't need no gold - en wings. ___
day turns in - to night, I hear my an - gel call - in' and I can't wait to see the light.
fe - ver com - in' o - ver me, I just hold my an - gel's hand and she puts me right back on my feet.
come down from the sky. Do like a good lit - tle an - gel and take me to par - a - dise.

hold _ _ _ _ _ _ _

Angel of Mercy – 7 – 2
PG9809

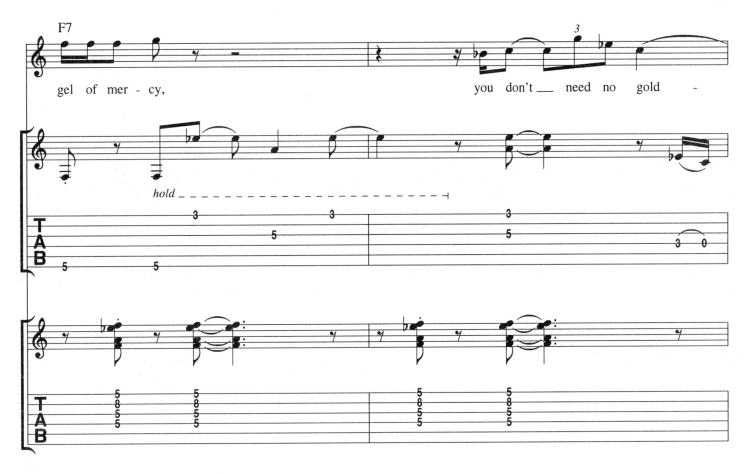

gel of mer - cy,     you don't ___ need no gold -

- en wings. ___     The way ___

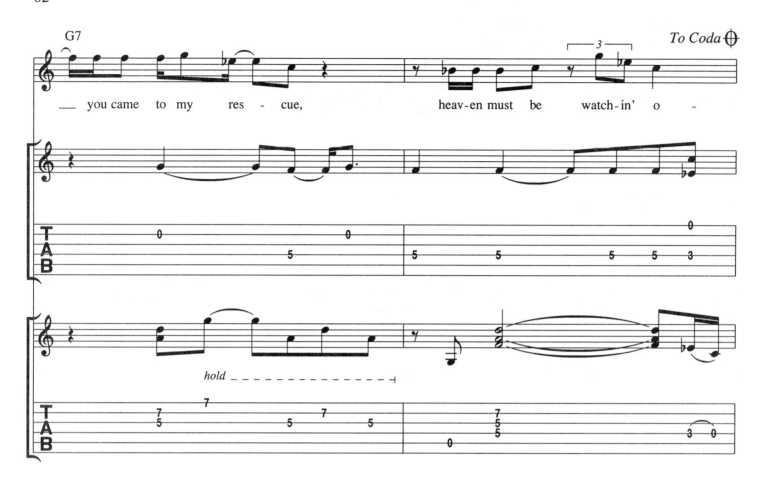

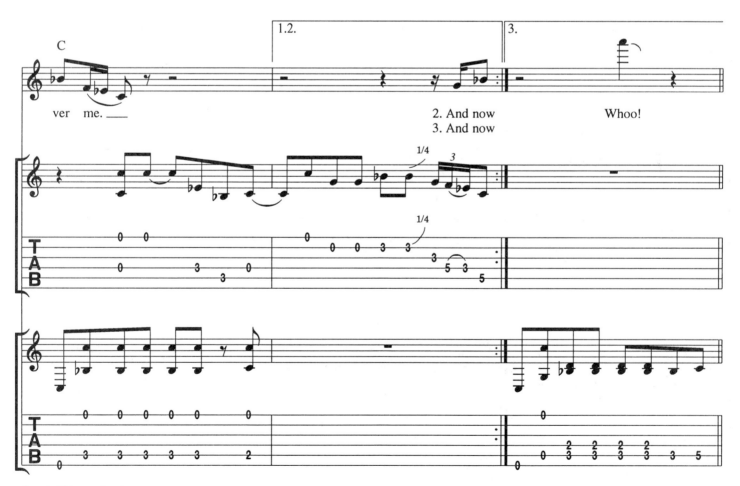

*Guitar Solo:*
*(Gtr. 2 use Verse as model for improv., 2 times)*

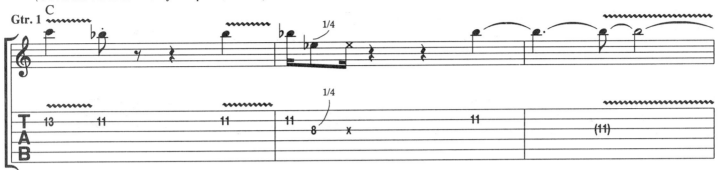

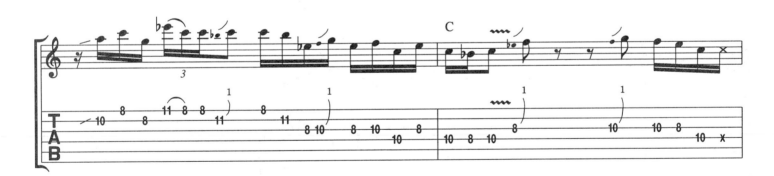

Angel of Mercy – 7 – 5
PG9809

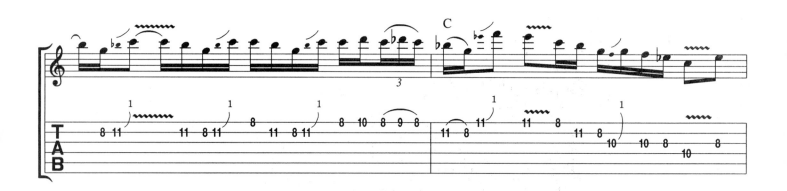

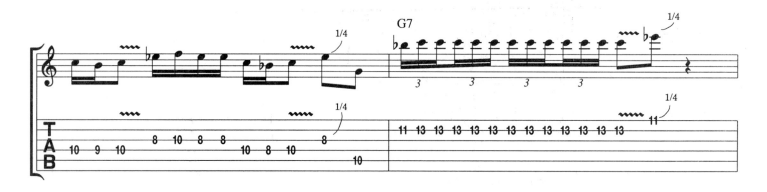

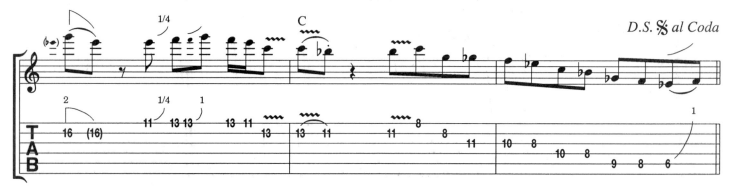

# RIGHT BACK

Words and Music by
DANNY KORTCHMAR and JERRY LYNN WILLIAMS

**Moderately fast** ♩ = 124

*Intro:*

Right Back – 7 – 1
PG9809

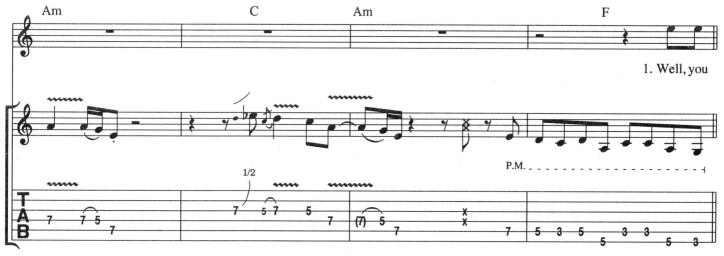

Pre-chorus:

You're mon-ey hun-gry and your heart is full of greed. ___

90

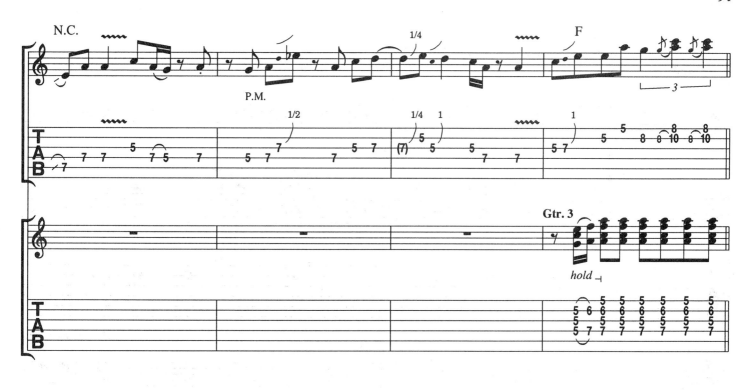

## Guitar Solo 2:

w/Rhy. Figs. 1 *(Gtr. 2)* & 1A *(Gtr. 3)* both 2 times
w/Riff A *(Gtr. 4)*

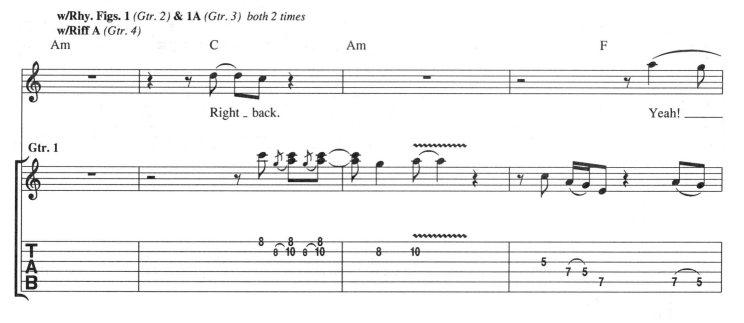

Right _ back.                                    Yeah! ____

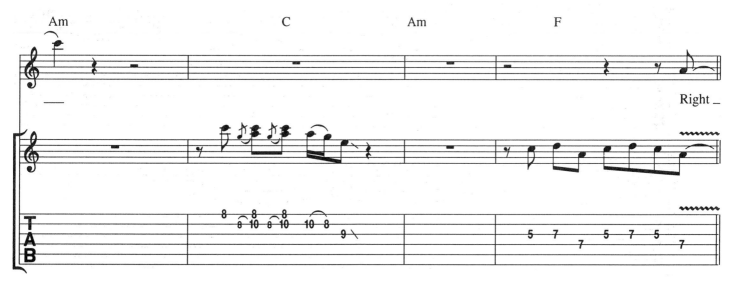

*Outro:*

# LEAVING TO STAY

Words and Music by
KEVIN BOWE

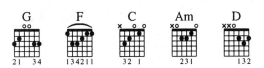

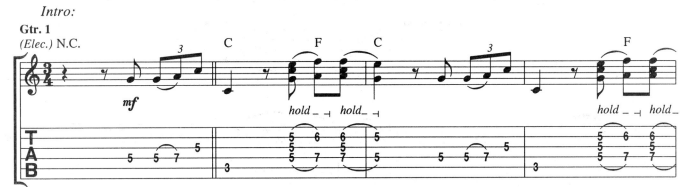

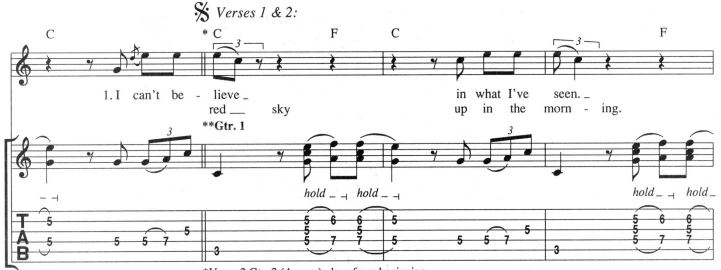

*Verse 2 Gtr. 2 (Acous.) plays from beginning.
**Gtr. 1 simile 2nd time.

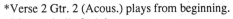

Leaving to Stay - 9 - 1
PG9809

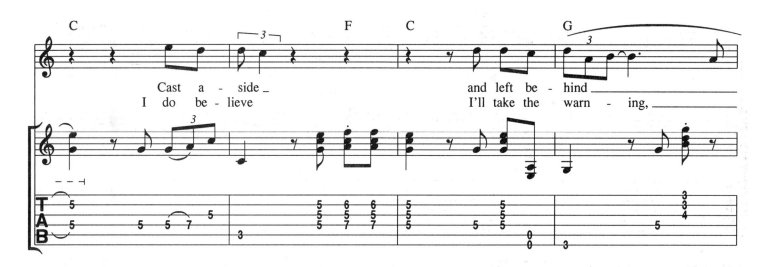

Cast a - side __ and left be - hind _____
I do be - lieve I'll take the warn - ing, _____

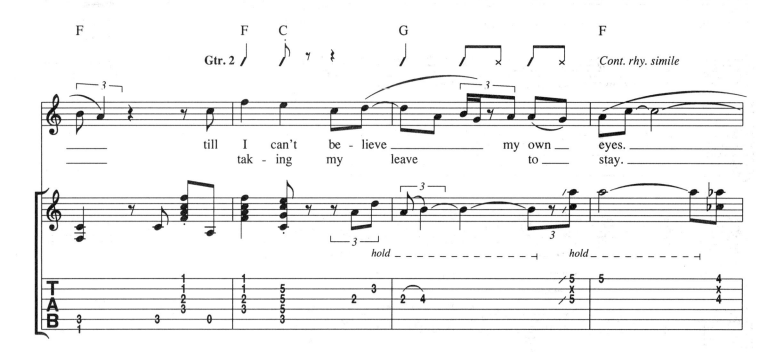

till I can't be - lieve __ my own __ eyes. _____
tak - ing my leave to __ stay. _____

Now, I been wait - ing for the glo - ry ___ of the com - ing of the

*To Coda I* ⊕

I'm fall-ing a - way. _____

**Gtr. 3**
*(Elec.)*

*f*

*pickup to Guitar Solo 1*

**Gtr. 1**

**end Rhy. Fig. 1**

*Guitar Solo 1:*

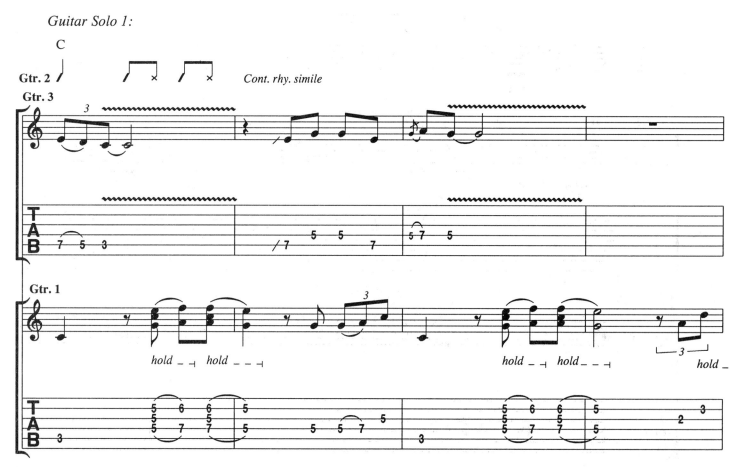

**Gtr. 2** *Cont. rhy. simile*

**Gtr. 3**

**Gtr. 1**

*hold* ⌐ *hold* ⌐ ⌐      *hold* ⌐ *hold* ⌐ ⌐      *hold*

# BEFORE YOU HIT THE GROUND

Words and Music by
JONNY LANG and KEVIN BOWE

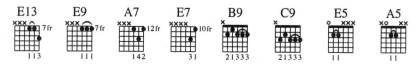

Moderately/funk ♩ = 90

*Intro:*

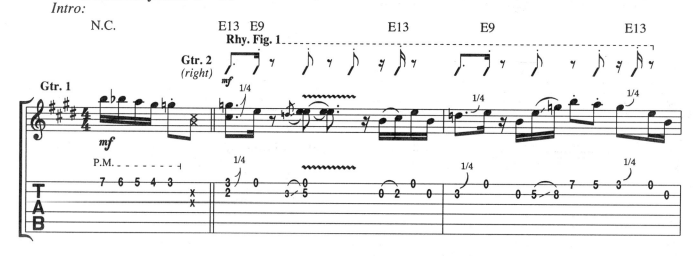

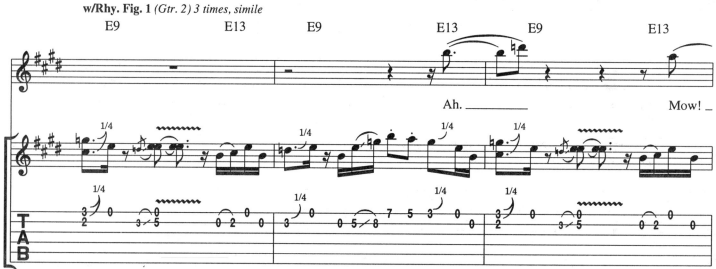

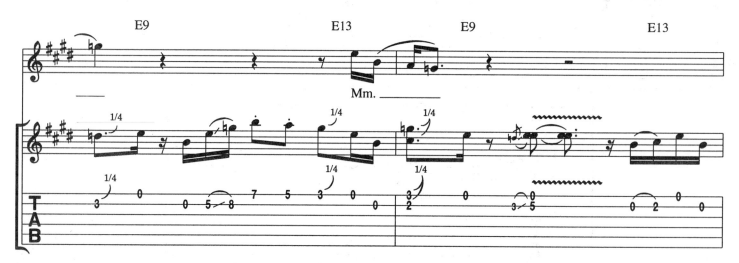

Before You Hit the Ground – 13 – 1
PG9809

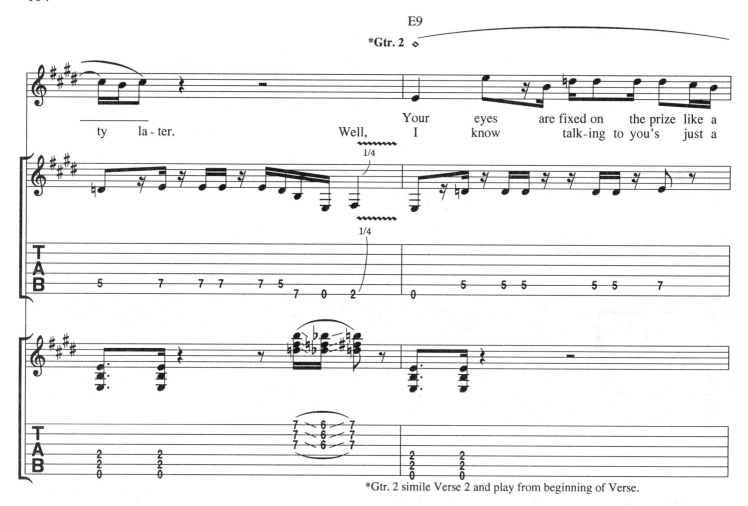

E9

*Gtr. 2

ty la - ter. Well, I know Your eyes are fixed on the prize like a

talk-ing to you's just a

1/4

1/4

*Gtr. 2 simile Verse 2 and play from beginning of Verse.

dead man's stare._____ Tick, tock, the hands on the clock don't
waste of my time._____ So I'm gon - na stop tell - in' you how to live your

1/2

*Bass/Band still playing A7.

2. w/Rhy. Fig. 1 *(Gtr. 2) 2 times, simile*

Ba - by, ow, be - fore you hit the ground.

Gtr. 5

110

Before You Hit the Ground – 13 – 9
PG9809

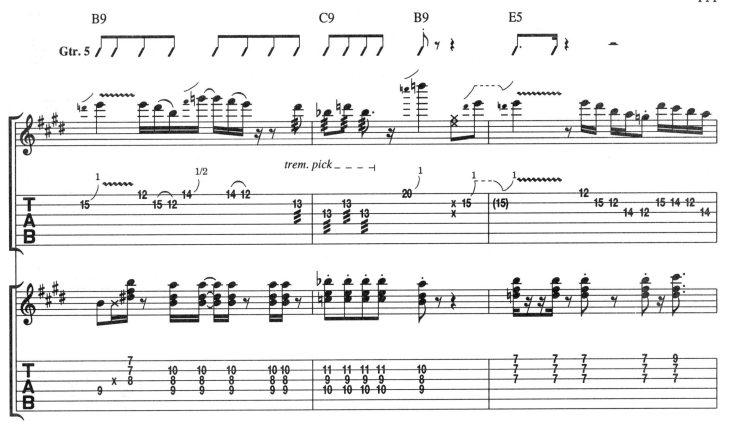

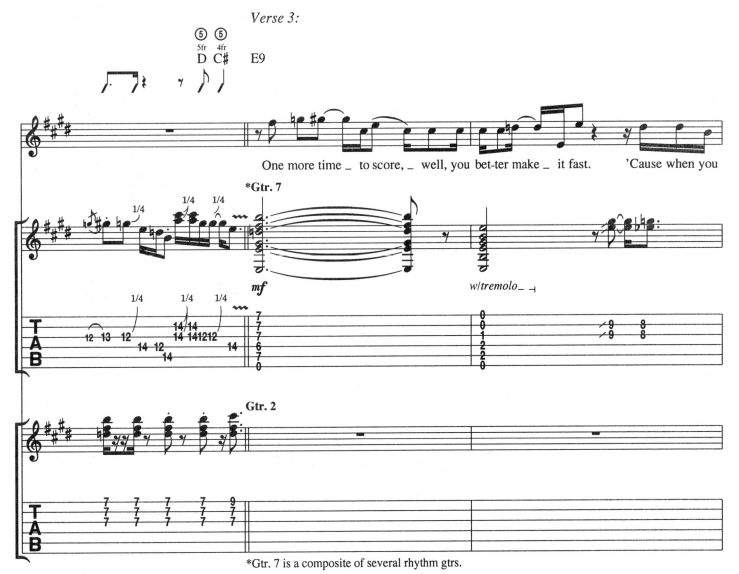

*Gtr. 7 is a composite of several rhythm gtrs.

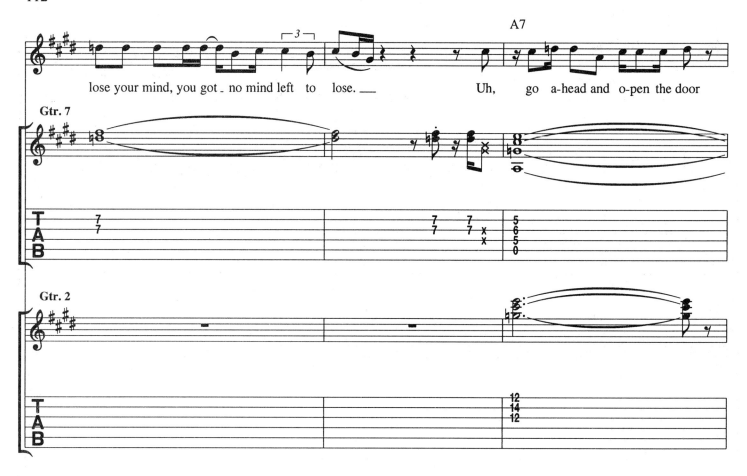

lose your mind, you got _ no mind left to lose. ___ Uh, go a-head and o-pen the door

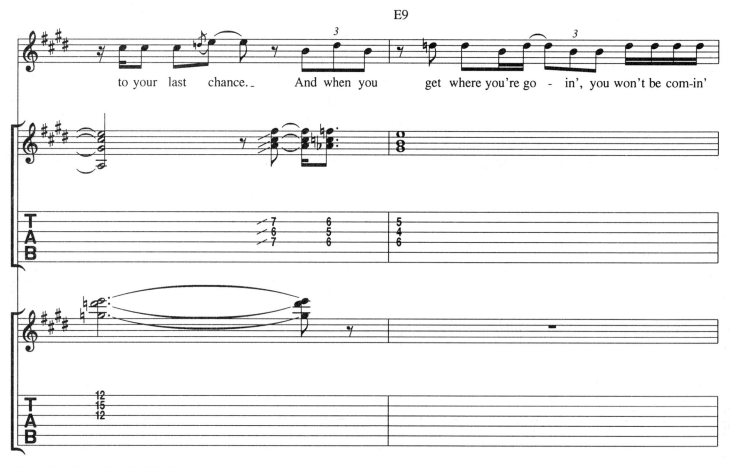

to your last chance. _ And when you get where you're go - in', you won't be com-in'

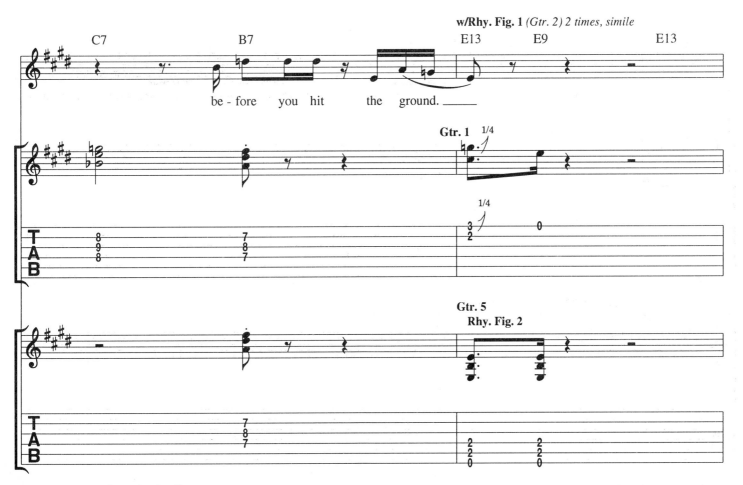

You got-ta hit the ground. _

(Spoken:) It don't feel too good.

end Rhy. Fig. 2

*Outro: w/ad lib. vocal*
**w/Rhy. Fig. 1** *(Gtr. 2) 5 times, simile*
**w/Rhy. Fig. 2** *(Gtr. 5) 2 times, simile*

**Gtr. 6**

*Begin fade*

**w/Rhy. Fig. 2** *(Gtr. 5) 1st 2 meas. only*

*Fade*

# CHERRY RED WINE

Words and Music by
LUTHER S. ALLISON

**Moderately slow** ♩. = 60

*Intro:*

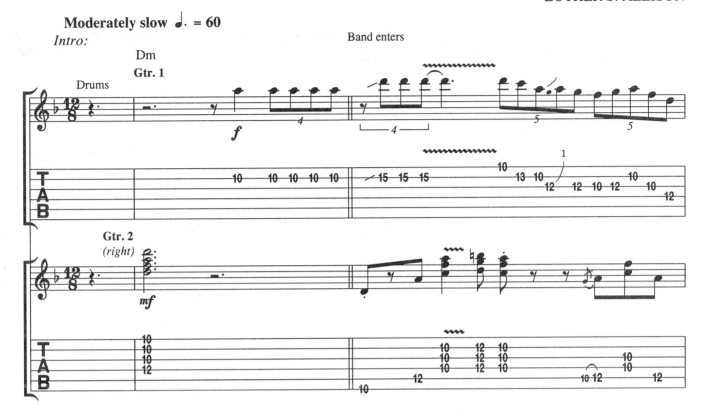

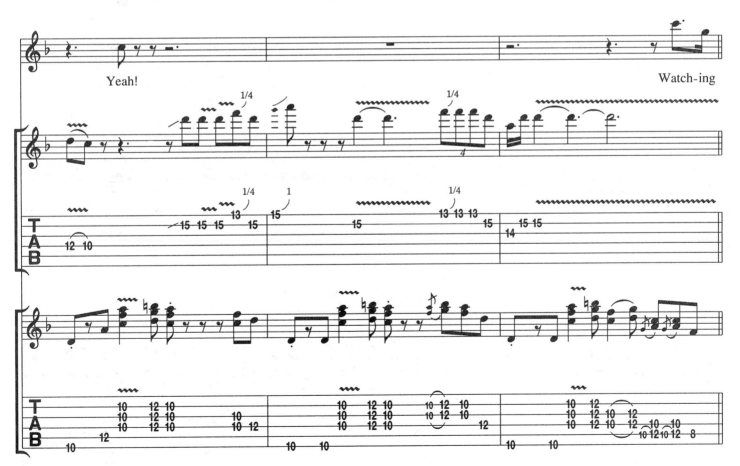

Cherry Red Wine – 8 – 1
PG9809

116

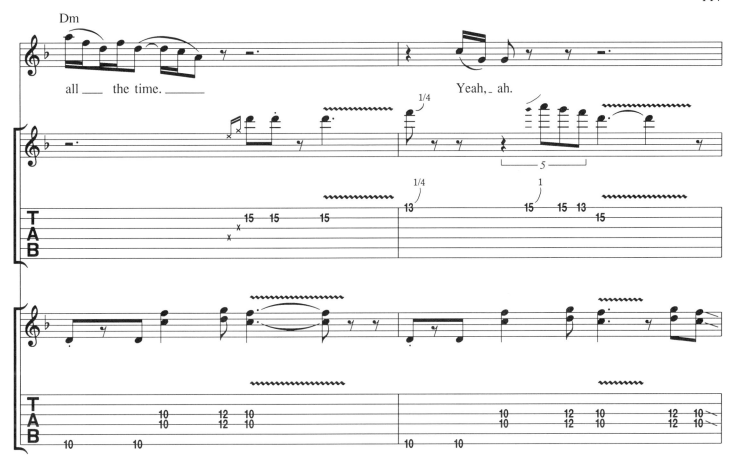

**Dm**

all ___ the time. _____ Yeah, _ ah.

**Am**

I'm watch-ing you de-stroy your-self _ now, wom-an,

**Gm**

while all you do is sit a-round drink-ing _

*hold _ _ _*

Cherry Red Wine – 8 – 3
PG9809

*Gtr. 1 Verse 2 only.
**Gtr. 1 Verse 3 only.

what can I do. ___ Yeah!
go-in' wrong in your head.

You're wor-ry-ing me, dar - ling.
I'm tak-ing  you to the doc - tor, wom-an.

I'm sit-tin' here won - der - ing _ what can I do. ___    Ah! _
May - be  the doc - tor   knows  what's  gone  wrong  in your head. Yeah, that's    right.

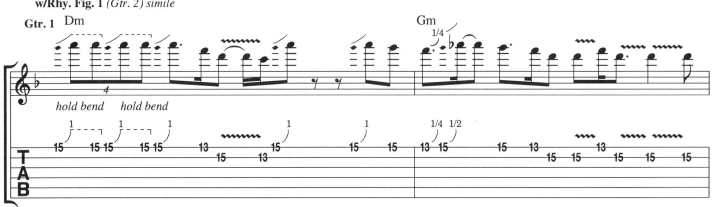

*Bend ① st. and ② st. at fret 15 with same finger.

wom-an,   e-ven the grass on your grave   will be cher - ry   red. _____

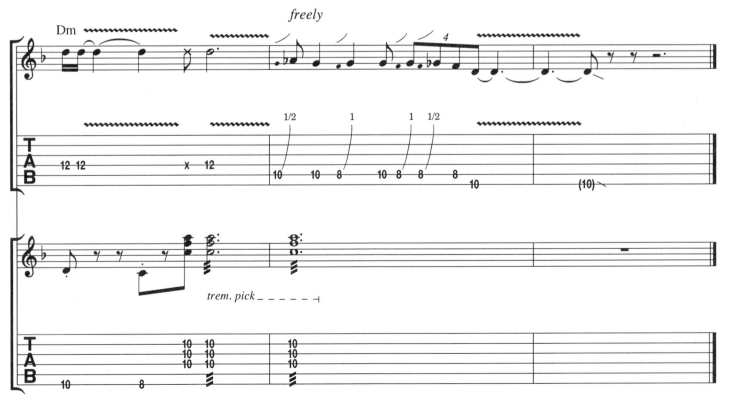

Cherry Red Wine – 8 – 8
PG9809

# GUITAR TAB GLOSSARY **

## TABLATURE EXPLANATION

**READING TABLATURE:** Tablature illustrates the six strings of the guitar. Notes and chords are indicated by the placement of fret numbers on a given string(s).

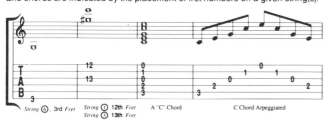

String ⑥, 3rd Fret    String ① 12th Fret    A "C" Chord    C Chord Arpeggiated
String ③ 13th Fret

## BENDING NOTES

**HALF STEP:** Play the note and bend string one half step.*

**WHOLE STEP:** Play the note and bend string one whole step.

**WHOLE STEP AND A HALF:** Play the note and bend string a whole step and a half.

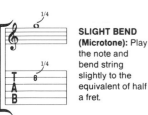

**SLIGHT BEND (Microtone):** Play the note and bend string slightly to the equivalent of half a fret.

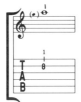

**PREBEND (Ghost Bend):** Bend to the specified note, before the string is picked.

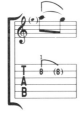

**PREBEND AND RELEASE:** Bend the string, play it, then release to the original note.

**REVERSE BEND:** Play the already-bent string, then immediately drop it down to the fretted note.

**BEND AND RELEASE:** Play the note and gradually bend to the next pitch, then release to the original note. Only the first note is attacked.

*A half step is the smallest interval in Western music; it is equal to one fret. A whole step equals two frets.

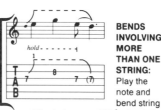

**UNISON BEND:** Play both notes and immediately bend the lower note to the same pitch as the higher note.

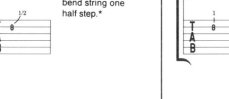

**DOUBLE NOTE BEND:** Play both notes and immediately bend both strings simultaneously.

**BENDS INVOLVING MORE THAN ONE STRING:** Play the note and bend string while playing an additional note (or notes) on another string(s). Upon release, relieve pressure from additional note(s), causing original note to sound alone.

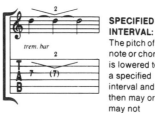

**BENDS INVOLVING STATIONARY NOTES:** Play notes and bend lower pitch, then hold until release begins (indicated at the point where line becomes solid).

## TREMOLO BAR

**SPECIFIED INTERVAL:** The pitch of a note or chord is lowered to a specified interval and then may or may not return to the original pitch. The activity of the tremolo bar is graphically represented by peaks and valleys.

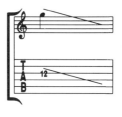

**UN-SPECIFIED INTERVAL:** The pitch of a note or a chord is lowered to an unspecified interval.

## HARMONICS

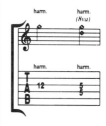

**NATURAL HARMONIC:** A finger of the fret hand lightly touches the note or notes indicated in the tab and is played by the pick hand.

**ARTIFICIAL HARMONIC:** The first tab number is fretted, then the pick hand produces the harmonic by using a finger to lightly touch the same string at the second tab number (in parenthesis) and is then picked by another finger.

**ARTIFICIAL "PINCH" HAR-MONIC:** A note is fretted as indicated by the tab, then the pick hand produces the harmonic by squeezing the pick firmly while using the tip of the index finger in the pick attack. If parenthesis are found around the fretted note, it does not sound. No parenthesis means both the fretted note and A.H. are heard simultaneously.

**By Kenn Chipkin and Aaron Stang

## RHYTHM SLASHES

**STRUM INDICATIONS:** Strum with indicated rhythm.

The chord voicings are found on the first page of the transcription underneath the song title.

**INDICATING SINGLE NOTES USING RHYTHM SLASHES:** Very often single notes are incorporated into a rhythm part. The note name is indicated above the rhythm slash with a fret number and a string indication.

## ARTICULATIONS

**HAMMER ON:** Play lower note, then "hammer on" to higher note with another finger. Only the first note is attacked.

**LEFT HAND HAMMER:** Hammer on the first note played on each string with the left hand.

**PULL OFF:** Play higher note, then "pull off" to lower note with another finger. Only the first note is attacked.

**FRET-BOARD TAPPING:** "Tap" onto the note indicated by + with a finger of the pick hand, then pull off to the following note held by the fret hand.

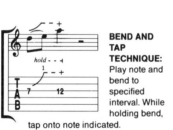

**TAP SLIDE:** Same as fretboard tapping, but the tapped note is slid randomly up the fretboard, then pulled off to the following note.

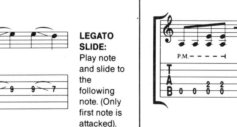

**BEND AND TAP TECHNIQUE:** Play note and bend to specified interval. While holding bend, tap onto note indicated.

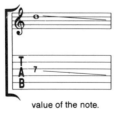

**LEGATO SLIDE:** Play note and slide to the following note. (Only first note is attacked).

**LONG GLISSANDO:** Play note and slide in specified direction for the full value of the note.

**SHORT GLISSANDO:** Play note for its full value and slide in specified direction at the last possible moment.

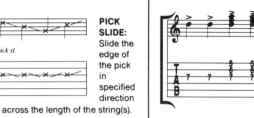

**PICK SLIDE:** Slide the edge of the pick in specified direction across the length of the string(s).

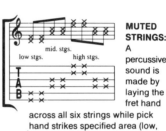

**MUTED STRINGS:** A percussive sound is made by laying the fret hand across all six strings while pick hand strikes specified area (low, mid, high strings).

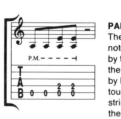

**PALM MUTE:** The note or notes are muted by the palm of the pick hand by lightly touching the string(s) near the bridge.

**TREMOLO PICKING:** The note or notes are picked as fast as possible.

**TRILL:** Hammer on and pull off consecutively and as fast as possible between the original note and the grace note.

**ACCENT:** Notes or chords are to be played with added emphasis.

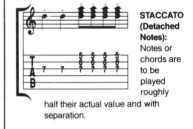

**STACCATO (Detached Notes):** Notes or chords are to be played roughly half their actual value and with separation.

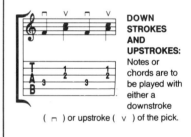

**DOWN STROKES AND UPSTROKES:** Notes or chords are to be played with either a downstroke ( ⊓ ) or upstroke ( ∨ ) of the pick.

**VIBRATO:** The pitch of a note is varied by a rapid shaking of the fret hand finger, wrist, and forearm.